Ben Helps

by Tim Little
Illustrated by Bill Ledger

OXFORD
UNIVERSITY PRESS

In this story ...

Ben

Ben can run as fast as a truck.

Miss Baker

Slink

3

Ben helps.

Miss Baker has a pot of cod.

Ben gets the pot.

Put it on the top.

Ben hits the bin and drops the pot.

Miss Baker tells Slink off.

9

Ben mops up the big mess.

It is not fun!